KELLY HOUSEMAN HEBERT
The Garden in My Mind

The Garden in my Mind
Kelly Houseman Hebert

Disclaimer

This book contains the ideas and opinions of its author. The intention of this book is to provide information, entertainment, helpful content, and motivation to young readers about the subjects addressed. It is published and sold with the understanding that the author is not engaged to render any type of psychological, medical, legal, or any other kind of personal or professional advice. This children's book is based on names, characters, places, and events which are products of the author's imagination. No warranties or guarantees are expressed or implied by the author's choice to include any of the content in this volume. The author shall not be liable for any physical, psychological, emotional, financial, or commercial damages, including, but not limited to, special, incidental, consequential, or other damages. The reader is responsible for their own choices, actions, and results.

1st Edition. 1st printing 2025

Cover and Illustrations: Illustrations Hub

Interior Design: Steve Walters, Oxygen Publishing Inc.

Independently Published
Oxygen Publishing Inc., Montreal, QC, Canada
www.oxygenpublishing.com

ISBN: 978-1-998686-02-5
Imprint: Independently published

Dedicated to my daughter, who is
kind, intelligent, and spunky.
The cutest little thing, with rainbow
sparkles in her eyes as she looks out into
the world, curly brown hair, and a smile
that is as bright as the shiniest star.

"Every thought-seed sown or allowed to fall into the mind, and to take root there, produces its own blossoming sooner or later into act, and bears its own fruit of opportunity and circumstance. Good thoughts bear good fruit, bad thoughts, bad fruit."

- As Man Thinketh, by James Allen
(Published in 1903)

Hi ya'll! I'm Camille Rose, but my friends call me Rosie.
My mom says I have an exceptional memory.

I can remember one time when I was 3 years old,
my mom and dad made me try broccoli and I spit it out!
I never let them forget this.

I remember what color t-shirt my mom was wearing
on the day of my kindergarten school parade.

And I remember the tiny marble I brought home from preschool that
I didn't play with for weeks - it mysteriously disappeared - my mom
promises it's packed away in the attic with all my other treasures.

My memory is so great that I don't forget anything - but especially the story of when I learned to be a gardener, but not just any gardener, a very special one that grows beautiful flowers. Do you want to hear how it all started?

Of course you do! You can grow flowers too with my gardening secrets.

It all started on a rainy-day during kindergarten.
I wasn't feeling like myself. I was driving to school with
my mom, and we always liked to sing songs in the car.
Except on this rainy day, I didn't feel like singing any songs.

I was worried. I had new worries. Things I never worried about before. Like what if no one wants to sit with me at lunch. Or what if my friends don't want to play with me outside. Or <gasp> what if I can't finish my math worksheets on time! There were so many worries, I felt like my head might pop off! And my stomach started to feel yucky.

I told my mom, and she said, "Oh my... you have
a visitor in your mind today. It's not a very kind
visitor, but she visits everyone. Even me. But if
we talk about her, she'll visit you less."

"What do you mean?!" I exclaimed. A visitor?
In my mind? Who could this be
and why is she there?

"Her name is Miss Imposter, and she likes to visit when kids start kindergarten," Mom explained. "Sometimes it's sooner, sometimes it's later." "She is pesky, she is known to interrupt you with unwelcomed visits when you least expect it."

"What does she look like?" I asked, my mind filled with curiosity.

"She's a tiny little thing," my mom said. "Kind of ugly I think, with crooked teeth and rumply clothes. But I'm not completely certain, most people don't see her with their eyes, they just hear her intrusive thoughts in their minds."

"What is an intrusive thought?" I asked.

"It's a thought that makes you feel like you can't do something, or that something bad might happen, or that someone might not like you," Mom said.

She continued, "Miss Imposter likes to trick us into believing lies - things about ourselves that just aren't true."

I felt off balance in my booster seat. How could this be? Has she been living in my mind all this time? Why is she there? Why does she want to make me believe lies?

My mom sensed my wonder, and asked, "Think about a garden. Flowers need certain conditions to grow and thrive. They need good soil, water, and plenty of sunshine."

"But weeds live in gardens too, and if we don't tend our gardens, water the soil and pull out the weeds, they can overtake the garden, growing too big and blocking the sunlight and the nutrients in the soil for the rest of the flowers," she explained.

I closed my eyes and tried hard to visualize a beautiful garden. It's a lot of work to make them look beautiful, pulling weeds is hard!

"Miss Imposter's thoughts are like weeds, Rosie.
Your mind is a big garden. Thoughts of 'I can do this'
and love and kindness towards yourself will grow
wildflowers and rose bushes."

Happiness

Thankful

Peace

love

A bright and sparkly light bulb lit up above my head. "I GET IT!" I yelled enthusiastically. "Miss Imposter plants weeds in my garden, so I need to yank them out, so they don't grow and block my flowers!"

"That's right!" my mom lovingly responded. "Everyone has a garden in their mind, they all look beautifully different, and we all have weeds that need to be tended to." I thought about this all day.

That night I took a bath, and as my mom brushed my hair, I started to feel worried about school the next day. My mom asked me if Miss Imposter tried to visit and plant any weeds while I was at school.

"No, not at school" I said, "but I think she's trying to plant weeds about school tomorrow, right now."

My mom put the brush down, and with a very
serious face started picking and combing through
my hair with her fingers. "Ah ha!" she yelled,
"I found a weed! Let's pull it out!"

My mom pulled the invisible weed right out and
together we looked for more. That night we found five
weeds that Miss Imposter planted, growing into worries.
We pulled them out and my mom tickled my head and
brushed my hair to make sure we had good soil
for my positive thoughts and big flowers the next day.
She watered them and reminded me how brave I was,
and how big of a heart I had in my chest.

ourage   Strength   Kindness   Calm

That night, as I laid in bed, I started to feel
the flower seedling roots take hold, by tomorrow
I was sure I would have all flowers, and no weeds.

The next day, we sang on the way to school. But when we got there, I started feeling worried. What if my friend didn't want to sit with me at lunch? What if my friends didn't like my new shoes? I was so excited for school, but now I didn't feel so sure. What if I forgot my animal facts during science class?

My tummy started to feel yucky.

But then, I remembered,
Miss Imposter had her grubby
gardener hands in my mind and
was planting weeds again! How
dare she! I know my friends love
sitting by me at lunch, and we
always laugh together. My shoes
look fantastic, and I know my
animal facts inside out.
Time to pull out your weeds,
Miss Imposter, my garden is
getting a lot of sunlight today!

Sometimes I didn't recognize Miss Imposter's presence, and weeds would start growing, my tummy would feel yucky, and I had trouble remembering that I needed to work on my garden. But with practice, I became a better gardener, and Miss Imposter's weed seeds didn't stand a chance.

My mom and I would talk about Miss Imposter when she came to visit. My mom said Miss Imposter visits her too! She said that a gardener's job is never done, but with enough practice you can recognize the weeds that need to be tended and the flowers that need more light and water.

When we talked about Miss Imposter, and practiced my gardening, I started to notice that the sunflowers in my mind garden grew a little taller, the bluebonnets looked a little more vibrant, and the daisies were blooming everywhere!

When I work on my garden, my tummy
feels yucky less often. When I pull out
Miss Imposter's weeds, there is
more room for flowers.

I told my friends about Miss Imposter.
They said she gets inside their gardens too!
Together we practice our weeding, and
when we tend our gardens together there
is ivy and rows and rows of rose bushes.
I saw a butterfly in there too, sitting
quietly on a flower and waiting for
me to notice its beautiful wings.

I'm all the way in 2nd grade now, and Miss Imposter still tries to grow weeds in my garden. I know that tending to my garden helps me be grateful for all the flowers that are there, and sometimes dealing with a little rain helps your flowers grow taller.

I keep pulling out the weeds, it's hard work, and it's never really done, but Miss Imposter knows that I don't tolerate her weeds for long.

I always remember to start pulling the weeds before they get too big, I take them out with the trash, and I focus on all the wild flowers and rose bushes that grow in my mind and flower around my heart.

ROSIE'S GARDENING SECRETS

1. Miss Imposter's weeds like dark and shady places. Spending time outside in the sun and laughing with family and friends helps bring in more light, and can be helpful for weeding.

2. Weeds grow quickly at night. Before bedtime, ask a loved one to help you prune them. Have them comb through your hair and yank out any plant growths that look suspicious. After they've been clipped and thrown away, have your loved one plant positive flower seeds and softly pat and massage them into your head. A little water helps for the positive seedlings too, have your loved one dance their fingers across your head like little droplets of water.

3. Eating fruits and vegetables help your mental flowers to grow taller, make sure you eat plenty of those for your garden.

4. Pulling weeds can be done anywhere at any time - sometimes they sneak up on you when you least expect it.

5. Gardening must be done regularly to prevent weed overgrowth; a gardener's work is never done!

ABOUT THE AUTHOR

Kelly Houseman Hebert is a mother, story-teller, and business strategist who believes in the power of metaphor to help children grow emotionally strong. When her daughter began experiencing anxiety in kindergarten, Kelly created a story on the car rides to school to help her name and navigate her feelings. That story became The Garden in My Mind.

Kelly lives in Texas, where she balances big picture business strategy with bedtime stories, cooking, and western horseback riding. Her mission is to help children (and their grown-ups) tend to the thoughts that take root and bloom.

Connect with Kelly:
📷 @KellyHebertWriting
Email: kchcollaborative@gmail.com
Website: kellyhebertwriting.com

The real life inspiration for Rosie.

www.ingramcontent.com/pod-product-compliance
Lightning Source LLC
Chambersburg PA
CBHW060815090426
42737CB00002B/68